IMAGES OF ENGLAND

CORSHAM

The Almhouses, Lacock Road, *c.* 1900.

IMAGES OF ENGLAND

CORSHAM

CORSHAM CIVIC SOCIETY

The
History
Press

First published in 1997 by the Chalford Publishing Company

Reprinted in 2011 by
The History Press
The Mill, Brimscombe Port,
Stroud, Gloucestershire, GL5 2QG
www.thehistorypress.co.uk

British Library Cataloguing in Publication Data
A catalogue record for this book is available from the British Library.

ISBN 978 0 7524 1071 5

Typesetting and origination by
The Chalford Publishing Company
Printed and bound in Great Britain by
Marston Book Services Limited, Didcot

Mr Bethel, nicknamed 'Finisher' Bethel as he never left a job half done, who was Corsham's last town crier. He is pictured here in the Meriton Avenue playground.

Contents

Foreword

As a member of the Corsham Civic Society I was pleased to have the opportunity to work with colleagues from the Photographic Society and compile a record of Corsham past. In this we benefited from the enthusiasm and expertise of those early photographers, diarist Herbert Spackman and eminent local architect Harold Brakspear. I was indebted to their families who kindly made their photographic collections available to me to copy. When approached by the Chalford Publishing Company we felt we should take the opportunity of sharing them with a wider audience. The original collection has been augmented by photographs and snapshots loaned to us by old Corsham families to whom we are very grateful. We are always interested in adding to the collection with a view to eventually opening a 'discovery centre' (as museums tend to be called these days), a place to discover the past in order to inform both present and future generations. If you should discover old photographs please allow the Society sight of them, as they may help to record or confirm the date on which events or changes have occurred in the town.

I hope you enjoy your journey into the days of Corsham past.

Tom Burnard
July 1997

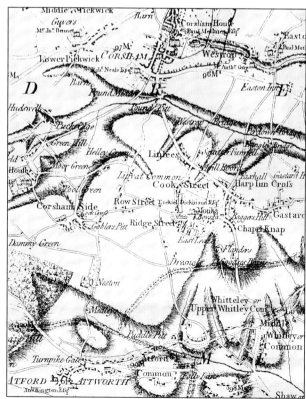

An early map of Corsham and surrounding area, charted b y ndrews and Dury in 1773.

Introduction

From earliest times the 'airy plateau' of Corsham seems to have been a desirable place to settle, with a Roman road to the south, extensive forests both south and west and a constant supply of clear spring water. Historian John Poulsom has uncovered evidence of Danish, Saxon and Celtic habitation particularly at Neston and Gastard. William the Conqueror must have been impressed as he gave the church and its lands to his favourite abbey at Caen. The town can surely claim to be the 'Cosham' or 'Cosseham' of the Anglo-Saxon chronicles. In 1015 here lay the ailing King Ethelred watching his 'ally', Eadric, raising an army only to be betrayed by the Knavish Ealdorman (alderman) so soon afterwards. Ethelred's 'palace' at Corsham was described by the twelfth century historian William of Malmesbury.

From Saxon times Corsham was a royal manor to which kings and consorts were no strangers. It became the property of King John's second son Richard, Earl of Cornwall, a crusader who was to become 'King of the Romans'. He ceded to the freemen of Corsham much of his land and considerable legal privileges in return for an annual rent of 110 marks.

Although a royal preserve, the deer in the great parks were a constant temptation to the adventurous. The assizes of 1305 record the trial of Richard de la Mere (ie. Monks), Walter of Westwells and two others for 'robbing Thomas De Taunton of a horse and goods to the value of £10 at Nettleton; robbing Henry Le King, vicar of Corsham, breaking the King's park at Corsham and there taking away twenty bucks and does against the peace'.

Woollen cloth manufacture dominated the following centuries. Perhaps encouraged by the policies of Edward III who spent the summer of 1346 in Corsham, local clothiers organised the various stages of the production of cloth which a national and international market. At the industry's peak there were three fulling mills on the little Ladbrook; all the other processes – carding, spinning, weaving, dying and finishing were conducted as a by-employment in the workers' cottages. Local wool was used, as well as that brought by pack-horse from the Cotswolds, and later fine-quality wool was imported from Spain. The clothiers arranged for the resulting broadcloth, and later the so-called 'medley' cloth, to be sent to the market in London. They prospered enough to build or refront several fine houses in the Corsham area in the seventeenth and early eighteenth century.

Corsham Court was rebuilt in 1582 by one 'Customer' Smyth, a Corsham man who found fame and fortune in London. During the Civil War it was the home of Sir Edward Hungerford, Commanding Officer of Cromwell's troops in Wiltshire who had a barracks at Westwells. His kindly temperament appears not to have contributed to any success as a soldier. His widow, Lady Margaret, left an indelible mark on the parish with the erection in 1668 of an impressive row of almshouses and a free school 'at the Town's End'.

The church of St Bartholomew is Saxon although Sir Harold Brakspear thought 'it quite possible that there was an even earlier church'. It has been enriched by considerable rebuilding over the centuries, although not always with the desired effect. In 1631 Dame Margaret Hungerford erected a gallery on the south wall and nine years later another was added on the opposite side. This led to the establishment of a full-time choir. A bitter controversy shattered the harmony and a stern letter from the Archdeacon of Wiltshire stated '..of late, some persons have taken upon them to oppose it (the choir) by singing in an opposite gallery a different tune to what is pitched by the said quire to the great dishonour of God and the disturbance of the congregation'. The galleries have long since disappeared, together with the controversy! Later building included that of a fine tower in the 1870s.

Corsham Court has been the seat of the Methuen family since 1745. Set in 600 acres of parkland, architects and landscape gardeners of the status of Ireson, Keene, Launcelot Brown,

The Old Market Hall, Corsham, 1873.

Wyatt, Nash, Repton and Bellamy have combined to make this one of the major Tudor/Gothic houses in the county. It safeguards the Methuen/Sanford collection of paintings, which includes rare Italian and Flemish works. The Court and gardens are open to the public.

By 1800 Corsham was in a poor state. There was little water for the water-power required once spinning and then weaving were mechanised, and there was no coal at all for steam-power. The Wiltshire cloth industry continued at Bradford and at Trowbridge, but Yorkshire was surging ahead. Change did not come to Corsham until Isambard Kingdom Brunel arrived to supervise the building of the phenomenal Box Tunnel between 1836 and 1841, which would complete his design for the Great Western Railway between London and Bristol. Four thousand navvies . . . .

Many an army has marched into the story of Corsham from Saxon to Dane and Roundhead. Here some of the Wiltshire Militia bivouacked during the Monmouth Rebellion and in 1903 Corsham played host to the manoeuvres of no less than 30,000 troops. Later years present a similar picture and in 1935 the War Office recognised the strategic potential afforded by the miles of abandoned stone mines. The technicians marched in and the now famous underground city came into being.

Today the march of time takes us, irrevocably, towards the dawn of a new century. If this little book from the Civic Society can cause you to pause and look back for a glimpse of the immediate past, or stir an echo of an earlier time, then it is worth remembering that a walk through Corsham is a walk through history. The path you tread can take you back to an age so distant that this millennium is but one.

The two sections of text in italics were contributed by Dr Negley Harte and augment the information in Joe James' original introduction.

Joe James
July 1997

One

South Place

South Place, c. 1955. A photograph taken by Alan Denhard, from the window of an upper room in The Warden's House, part of the Lady Margaret Hungerford Almshouses.

A team of Peter Sellars lookalikes? Cricket has been enjoyed in Corsham since 1848, although in those early times, only after 'haying time' was completed. In this Victorian group the thatched pavilion can just be seen in the background. Three of the Spackman brothers are included in the team. Clair (front left) was the bowler who once dismissed the great W.G. Grace for a duck! The other seated figure on the right is S.P. (Sep) Kinnear, the second Corsham-born cricketer to play for England. (The other was the fast bowler Jim Smith who played for Middlesex.)

A mixed match in the 1940s. Are the ladies still allowed onto the pitch once a year? Back row: -?-, -?-, Frank White, -?-, Dennis Hazel, Bill Gale, -?-, Reg Pullin, Harold Gale. Middle row: Madge Hutton, Pat Aust, -?-, Marjorie Knapp, -?-, -?-. Front row: -?-, Pat Smith, Audrey McEwen, Doris White, Mavy Miflin. This year the club celebrated their 150th anniversary and finished the 1997 season as Champions of the County Alliance League Division II.

The Corsham cricket ground. The parish rooms can be seen in the background of this original Spackman photograph. Whether the occasion was a fancy dress cricket match or social, the authors can only surmise. The Corsham news reported in 1888: 'A movement is on foot to form a tennis club in the town. The committee of the Cricket Club met at the Town Hall on Thursday evening to consider an application for the hire of a portion of the cricket field. Mr T.P. Stevens presided. The committee after discussion decided to let a part of the field for a tennis court on the condition that it should be an open club and that the members should not play during a cricket match'.

A Spackman original photograph showing a mixed group at the Corsham bowling green, 4 October 1918.

S. JOHN'S AMBULANCE ASSOCIATION.

Among the many societies formed in Corsham in connection with politics, music, temperance, literature and art, we have not had in our midst for many years a society of such a scientific nature as the branch of the above association, recently formed in the town. Several ladies in the neighbourhood having expressed a desire to form a class, Dr. J. Ellis Crisp, M.R.C.S., kindly promised to conduct a series of lectures if a sufficient number of members could be got together. A strong class of 26 ladies has now been formed, and they meet weekly at the Townhall. The main objects of the association are :—(a) The dissemination of instruction in "first aid," i.e., the preliminary treatment of the sick and injured pending the doctor's arrival. (b) Lectures to women on home nursing and hygiene. (c) The deposit in appropriate localities of material (such as stretchers, hampers, splints, bandages, &c.) for use in case of accident. (d) The development of ambulance corps for the transport of the sick and injured. Since the institution of the movement in 1877, many hundreds of "Detached" classes, and 250 "Centres" have been formed in all parts of the world, and upwards of 90,000 certificates of proficiency have been awarded. Instances of efficient "first aid" rendered by certificated pupils are of almost daily occurrence, and numerous cases, corroborated by the highest medical testimony, have been reported to S. John's Gate, and are there registered, certifying that life has been saved by pupils through the application of the knowledge acquired. The dangerous nature of the occupation of the large majority of the working classes in the stone quarries all around, renders the formation of such a class a greater necessity in this locality than in many of the neighbouring towns, but though these workmen are naturally exposed to accidents they possess no monopoly of danger. The country gentleman may as easily break a leg or a collar bone in the hunting field as the ordinary foot passenger treading on a cabbage leaf or a piece of orange peel on the pavement may slip and dislocate an ankle. Even a simple act, such as breaking the glass when drawing the cork from a bottle, may cut an artery and inflict such an injury that life will be lost unless immediate steps be taken to arrest the bleeding. A child can do this if properly taught, and, as Dr. Crisp pointed out, a simple fracture very often becomes complicated, and fatal results ensue through the ignorance of those who give the first aid to the injured. At the first lecture, on Friday last, Dr. Crisp in his preliminary remarks, explained the objects of instruction, and then gave a general outline of the structure and functions of the human body, including a brief description of the bones, muscles, arteries, and veins, the functions of the circulation, respiration, and of the nervous system. He also explained the application of the triangular bandage. At the second lecture, on Tuesday, Dr. Crisp traced the general direction of the main arteries, indicating the points where the circulation may be arrested by digital pressure, or by the application of a tourniquet, and explained the difference between arterial, venous, and capillary bleeding, and the various extemporary means of arresting it. Two lads consented to submit themselves to the tender mercies of the fair amateurs, and thus the practical illustration of the lecturer's remarks were greatly facilitated. Dr. Crisp expressed himself highly gratified with the progress of the class.

A St John's Ambulance article of 1888.

A stylish gathering of ladies but Herbert Spackman has given neither date nor reason for recording the occasion. Perhaps this is indicative that it is one of his earlier photographs. Could they possibly be the ladies referred to in the article to the left?

A Spackman original of the British Red Cross Society and St John's Ambulance Association, sometime before the First World War.

The Corsham St John's Ambulance Association, grouped behind the Mansion House, July 1945. For a number of years they met in the cricket pavilion, The Corsham branch of St John's have recently acquired the redundant telephone exchange in Alexandra Terrace and go into the millennium with a permanent base in which to meet. Back row: Dolly Lodge, Dorothy Newell, Betty Hancock, Amelia Lewis, Joan Fuller, -?-, Moya Wyatt. Third row: Betty Harris, Ruby Davis, Mrs Cleverly, Greta Simmons, Eva Love, Grace Ponting, Irene Tilley, Winnie Allen, -?-. Second row: Ethel Smith, Kathy Newell, Doris Smith, Sister Williams, Dr Wheeler, Mrs Kelshaw, Mrs Wheeler, Vi Barnes, Sybil Gadd, Olive Gale, Mrs Norton. Front row: -?-, -?-, Doreen Allen, Barbara Jones, Thelma Lodge, Marjorie Knapp, Pam Bryant, Myra Elms, Doris Horton, Sheila Sawyer, Jo Phelps, -?-, -?-, -?-, -?-.

Horsefair Cottage, No.3 Station Road, August 1966, from the NMRC collection at Swindon. A charming corner of Corsham.

The National Church Mission listening to an address from the vicar outside 'The Grove', 14 October 1916.

Steven Hill was a fixture at the junction of Station Road, High Street and Pickwick Road, sitting on a box which he kept beside the wall of The Grove, directing horse-drawn traffic. He had a crippled leg and lived in Paul Street. He died prior to the Second World War, perhaps before the increased speed and number of motor vehicles made his life too hazardous!

The Challenge Shield of the Wiltshire Choral Competition was won by the Corsham Choral Society for three years in succession, at Warminster, Swindon and Salisbury in 1908, 1909 and 1910 respectively. On the third occasion it was presented to them in perpetuity and today hangs in the library. The Choral Society was reformed some twenty years ago and met at The Grove. They now meet at Corsham Town Hall each Wednesday evening at 7.30 p.m. and new members are assured of a warm welcome.

A Spackman plate negative showing the Corsham Choral Society at 'The Grove', 18 July 1900.

The insert to the right shows the sign of the 'Chequers' either side of the door, in the south wall of the Methuen Arms.

The Methuen Arms

John Aubrey claimed a nunnery once occupied this site and a drawing by Buckler of 'Winters Court' may suggest ecclesiastical overtones but it has not been possible to substantiate this beyond doubt, or that the Methuen Arms was founded in 1417. It is known the previous building was owned by the Nott family and a rumbustious member, Christopher, attempted to open an alehouse in 1608.

'The homage within the libertie of Corsham hath often times made presentments that three tippling houses are enough and sufficient.... that is to say Thos Rolfe, vintner, John Merrett, innholder and Giles Keynes, butcher. Notwithstanding Christopher Nott hath about a year since sett up a new alehouse in a remote place in the skirts of the towne, where is dayle used great abuses by drunkards, common haunters of alehouses and idlers. That the said Nott be lately presented for setting a rayle and straightening the highway hath made in contempt of the said presentement sett up the sygne of the Red Lion. The court ordered the alehouse to be suppressed'

But the 'Red Lion' survived, although the survival of the landlord is little short of miraculous. Christopher was acquitted of fighting a customer John Coryn of Wraxall, but fined 9d. for injuring Thomas Little. In 1613 he was arrested for playing cards on the Sabbath, later for selling 'spiced bread' with Widow Keynes. The lady was described as a 'night walker'!

Datestones on the south wall of the hotel (difficult to see from the Lacock Road) inform of the transfer from the Notts to their descendant, Elizabeth Webber, then to her daughter Christian in 1749, the last of the line. In the 1930s a lady purchased an antique dog collar in Bath. The inscription thereon read: 'Elizabeth Webber at the Red Lion. Corsham, Wilts 1749'.

In 1779 Christian died and the ownership was acquired by the Methuen family in the late eighteenth century. The 'Red Lion' became the 'Methuen Arms' in 1805 and much rebuilding was commissioned. The skittle alley, patronised by the Duke of Edinburgh during his period of service at HMS Royal Arthur, was once a brewhouse and malting. After the posting trade died, the Methuen Arms was a hunting inn with stabling for forty horses. A door in the south wall displays the 'chequers' sign, an indication of a 'hostelry' as far back as the days of ancient Pompeii.

Mr Fred Fuller at the Metheun Arms, c. 1910. As the testimonial on the following page indicates, he was held in great esteem by his employers, Mr and Mrs Ogburn. His daughter, Mrs Joan Moon, had glowing references in her possession and we have chosen that written by Harry V. Lloyd.

METHUEN ARMS HOTEL,
CORSHAM, WILTS.

TELEGRAMS
"METHUEN ARMS,"
CORSHAM.
TELEPHONE N° 39.

Sept 17 191

Dr Mr Fuller,

Just a line to say how truely sorry I to part with you, further I shall always be at your service as a friend, and will give, both personal & written testimonial to any one wishing same for you During the years I have known you "since 1911" I have proved you to be the soul of honor & good principal, and your devoted duty to my

dear Niece's interest in every detail of the business, since her husband joined up in 1915 has won my thanks and admiration —

May good luck attend you in your future Again I say, if ever I can be of any service to you, please command me and believe me

Yours Sincerely
Harry. V. Lloyd

Central News
Irish Club
Charing Cross Road
London
W.C.

The testimonial written by Mrs Ogburn's uncle, Harry V. Lloyd.

Mrs Ogburn and Mr Fuller about to depart from the Metheun Arms in the pony and trap, a favourite photograph which Mr Fuller always carried in his wallet. He had the sad task of closing the hotel in 1917 when he himself joined the Army and Mrs Ogburn was unable to continue to run such a large establishment on her own.

The workforce of Osborne & Sons, 1933. Here they are pictured in the car park of the Metheun Arms (the wall in the background being that of the old Corsham Fire Station). Osborne & Son were established in 1755 and continued to carry out much of the work to the larger houses in the district until the death of Mr Bert Osborne in the early 1960s. In those days loyalty was appreciated and Arthur Gingell worked with them for thirty-one years as a sawyer (sixth right in the back row). Top row: Arthur Newbury, Bill Frankham, Billy Hatter, Bob Oatley, Fred Gale, Bob Wright, George Chamberlain. Centre row: Vernon Cole, Joe Dew. Front row: Stanley Osborne, Carl Buckle, Ted Say, Bill Taylor, Ernie Cole, Billy Brown, Jack Lumpkins, Ken Lumpkins, Frank Fletcher, Bob Lambridge, Alf Reed, Billy Fry, Bill Young, Henry Williams, Lawrence Waite, Walter Baker, Jim Mines, Jack Simmons, Bert Osborne.

Two

Pickwick Road to Pickwick

Pickwick Road, September 1907. Corsham celebrates the coming of age of the Hon. Paul A. Methuen.

On the corner of High Street and Pickwick Road, c. 1963, J.H. Harding ran a business established in 1889 by Thomas Fowler Harding which later became Harding & Son. During the 1930s, Mr Shepherd was manager but in 1948, Mr Box succeeded him. It was during this time that a nephew of Mr J. Harding, a Mr George Carson, began working there, eventually taking control of the business. The Harding family served the people of Corsham for eighty years.

It is called progress!

Can you identify these photographs? George Hales, a coachman at Shockerwick House, (an upright, self-righteous man who never lost his cockney accent) eventually set up a garage business in nearby Station Road. He and his wife gave a home to a young orphan who, just nine years old, was travelling from Australia on a German tramp steamer when war broke out in 1914. She, Miss Winnie Weekes, later became a teacher at the Methuen School and was a keen member of the Drama Society.

Another view of what became a Chinese takeaway and to its right, a taxi service. More recently the house has returned to residential use after the owner gained permission to create a prestigious gated housing development in the yard to the rear.

1963 – to the left is Pickwick Papers, now Oatleys. A Mr Fricker, then a Mrs Reeves, traded there unitl 1939. 'Daddy' Reeves was known as one of the finest furniture restorers in the country. (A glimpse also of the cottages on the right, demolished when the precinct was built in the 1970s).

Troops in the First World War passing through Corsham, along Pickwick Road.

CHRISTMAS IN THE SHOPS.—The shop windows in the town, as we write, are beginning to wear a very Christmas-like appearance. Mr. W. H. Beszant is making a grand display of beef, mutton and poultry. Included in the show are eight very prime maiden heifers, grazed by Mr G. P. Fuller, M.P., Neston Park; four choice steers, grazed by Sir John Dickson Poynder, Hartham; three superior heifers, grazed by Mr. Wm. Crook, of Binegar; these choice specimens were prize-takers at the Melksham Cattle Show. Coming to the mutton, ten choice wether sheep fed by Mr. W. J. Long, of Rowden farm, Chippenham, are deserving of special notice, and also ten prime Southdowns, grazed by Mr. D. E. Holbrow, Castle Combe. Mr. Beszant's selection also includes five Southdowns, grazed by Mr Minett, Easton, and three choice old wethers, grazed by Mr. W. Crook, of Binegar (first prize-takers at Melksham Cattle Show), and a prime fat calf, fed by Mr. John Bovy, Castle Combe. There is also a collection of poultry. Mr. Coates, as usual, makes a specially good display of turkeys and geese. His selection this year includes some remarkably fine birds from Mr. Leonard, of Sheldon farm, and Miss Anstey, Notton farm, and some choice geese from Mr. Milsom, Wick farm, and Mr. Minty, Cartridge farm. There are also two prime oxen grazed by Mr. Breach, Binegar, and one from Mr. Large, Swindon. Mr. Coates has purchased over a hundred head of poultry, and his show equals, if not surpasses, that of previous years. Mr. Carter also has some well-selected beef and mutton, and the other shops of the town make suitable show windows for the Christmas season. The principal drapers and some of the grocery establishments are to be closed from this evening (Saturday) till Thursday morning.

This display in Pickwick Road is referred to in the newspaper article of 1888. No fear of BSE it seems. Each butcher knew where his stock had been grazed and by whom!

Marsh & Son, *c.* 1900. Many are those who wonder where 'the fish' is now. 'Rockie' Marsh as he was known not only sold fresh fish and vegetables, but also fried fish and chips. As a sideline he also cleared houses and sold both furniture and clothes to Corsham families. Mr Fricker, whose father ran a shop a few doors away, described Rockie Marsh as the original Walcot Reclamations!

A photograph taken by Richard Morling of Pickwick Road, 1963.

Bullock, watch and clock maker, *c.* 1890. This business was established in the early 1840s by Thomas and continued in the name of Stephen Bullock from the late 1880s until a little before the close of Edward VII's reign. (Note the clock face just below the roof line and the bay windows). The Bullocks traded for over sixty-five years. Was this a photograph of Thomas, Stephen, or a satisfied customer?

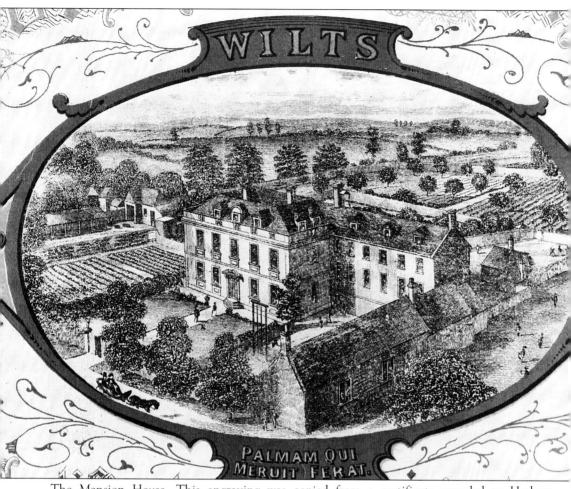

The Mansion House. This engraving was copied from a certificate awarded to Herbert Spackman for 'Proficiency in French Class II' in July 1877. Charles H. Hulls was the Principal. For further reading see pages 3 and 4 of Herbert Spackman's *A Corsham Boyhood*. The Mansion House was built between 1721 and 1724 by the Neale family, clothiers of Yate. The cellars were said to contain stone vats used for dyeing cloth. It became a school for boys in Victorian times and notable pupils included Richard Bethel, who became Lord Westbury the Lord Chancellor, and Reginald Younghusband who showed great bravery as an officer in the wars against Chief Cetewayo at Isandula in South Africa. It has been a youth centre since the late 1940s and more recently has provided accommodation for a crèche and playschool. As we go to print the building and its land are to be sold by Wiltshire Council.

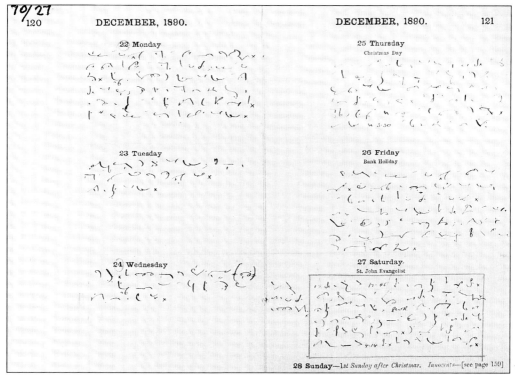

22 Monday

23 Tuesday

24 Wednesday

25 Thursday
Christmas Day

26 Friday
Bank Holiday

27 Saturday.
St. John Evangelist

28 Sunday—1st Sunday after Christmas. Innocents—[see page 159]

An extract from Herbert Spackman's diary,
December 1890. It was recorded in meticulous
Pitman's shorthand.

A detailed study of the window and date stone
at the Mansion House taken by the Wiltshire
Buildings Record, 1982. 'N.R.S.' 1723, refer to
the first occupants, Robert and Sarah Neale.

A 1963 photograph by Richard Morling. The hut to the right at the end of the pathway being Little's Fish & Chip shop, popular with hungry patrons of the cinema. This photograph records that demolition work had commenced, which would eventually enable Newlands Road to be created. The pedestrianisation of the southern end of the High Street followed.

The Regal Cinema, Corsham.

Early in 1930, Osborne & Sons (builders) were seen to be laying the foundations of a substantial building in Pickwick Road. Word soon got around that the town was about to have its own cinema. This was duly opened later in the year by Mr Andrews, a fairground operator who, although stone deaf, coped well with the innovation of the 'talkies', helped by his sons. The town flocked to see Bebe Daniels sing her way through *Rio Rita* and also an obscure singer in the *King of Jazz* called Bing Crosby. The same stairs served both balcony and projection room, the door of which was usually left open. As they passed, most patrons would shout 'Hello Nels!' and Nels would bob up from behind the gleaming projectors to return the greeting.

In 1935 a new owner, Mr Stratford, added Corsham to others in his Cotswold circuit. He renamed the cinema 'The Regal', a nod, no doubt, to Corsham's royal past, and assisted by his wife and daughter (now Mrs Tilley), the best that Paramount and MGM could offer graced the local screen.

For the technical, the equipment consisted of 'Kalee Seven' projectors linked to Morrison pull-through sound heads. The projectionist's dread was the failure of the rectifying valve, which supplied the current for the arc lamps. No switch-over facilities were available, so the show had to be interrupted for a few minutes while the large valve of boiling mercury was replaced. To save warm-up time the current was never switched off, so the operation was as hazardous as it was uncomfortable. Behind the sound proofing of the projection room the operators were fortunately oblivious of the inevitable cat-calls from the hall, just as the audience were equally unaware of the palm sweating activity behind the scenes!

In 1958 Norman and June Jeffries took over the cinema and in 1969 Norman, using his own building skills, enlarged the accommodation and added a modern foyer to the re-named 'Corsham Film Theatre'.

The theatre ran for a further fifteen years, the curtains finally closing in 1985. Today as TV brings yesterday's films to a new and wider audience many local people recall the time when they first saw the same epic from the stalls of the little cinema in Pickwick Road.

Joe James
Once the projectionist at the Regal Cinema

In 1935 fountain pens, or pen and ink, were widely used so Mr Stratford advertised each month's films on blotting paper in expectation of its being in constant daily use.

Wood's Glove Makers, June 1934. The girls used to work in the wooden building immediately to the right as one turns into Paul Street from Pickwick Road, (now Unwins Upholsterers). Back row: ? Trotman, Dorothy Payne, Nancy Moody, Lucy Fisher, Doris Gosling. Kneeling: Nellie Gray, Peggy Moody, Cath Phelps, Mary Cainey, Bet Potter, Monica Gale, Mary Smith.

Paul Street. Nellie and Stanley Gibbons, pictured with their grandfather, in the garden of his Paul Street home.

George F. Gibbons, pictured beside his exhibits at a local show, his sister-in-law is on the right, *c.* 1904. A keen bee-keeper he regularly judged entries at shows around the county.

A view of Corsham taken from the top of the fire appliance ladder in 1963 by Richard Morling. The black building is the original library where Lynette Bowman served the people of Corsham prior to the construction of the present library built to the east of the Mansion House.

Edwin Merrett (with bicycle) and his wife, Selina, to his right, standing outside their home and business in Pickwick Road. (Edwin's forefathers established the Merrett building business in 1843 and two roads in Corsham bear their name, Erneston Crescent and Meriton Avenue. Other properties are to be found in Paul Street, Pickwick Road and Alexandra Terrace). The photograph shows Edwin and Selina with son Ernest standing to the right of the double gate. His daughter-in-law Lily Merrett, (wife of son Walter with a garage business in the High Street), is nearest the trap and his daughter Elsie is sitting in the trap. The workman on the left of the gate is Norman Say.

The daughters of Walter and Lily Merrett, Connie and May, kept a fruit and vegetable shop next door to their father's garage. Ernest had three daughters, Greta, Violet and Cynthia. Greta became Mrs Gorton whose husband managed a dairy round bearing his name. Violet became Mrs Herbert Merrett, and it was he (see page 38) who continued the business of builder and funeral director. Cynthia took an interest in the business of her husband until her father's death then took to caring for her mother, Rosina, who died in the February of her hundredth year. Rosina was the daughter of Mr and Mrs Jack Simmons, pictured on the next page.

Mr Francis Simmons and his wife Charlotte of South Street.

Selina and Edwin Merrett, *c.* 1890.

The Merrett's funeral hearse pictured in Pickwick Road.

The Merrett's wedding coach also pictured in Pickwick Road, which they let out on hire.

Rosina and Ernest's three daughters, *c.* 1917. From left to right: Greta, Violet and Cynthia.

A for sale notice marks the end of an era for Snells, the blacksmith's shop, *c.* 1970. This is now the site of the Jet garage.

Three

Pickwick

One car in Pickwick! This photograph from the NMRC collection has no date but entered their collection in 1943, attributed to John Winstone. The vehicle suggests it was taken sometime around the 1930s.

The Hare and Hounds public house and the Moses Pickwick story. It is interesting to note the advertisement on the south wall: 'Good accommodation for cyclists'. Notice also the unusual square weathervane on the gable end.

Sir Frederick Goldney (1845–1940) lived at nearby Beechfield House. He was High Sheriff of Wiltshire in 1908, having been twice Mayor of Chippenham. He was well regarded as an employer and landlord and is reputed to have distributed 'rounds of beef' to tenants at Christmas time.

PARTICULARS.

THE WELL-KNOWN AND HIGHLY POPULAR

FREE FULLY-LICENSED PREMISES

known as

"THE HARE AND HOUNDS,"
PICKWICK.

The Accommodation includes :—

On the Ground Floor :—

BAR, BOTTLE AND JUG DEPARTMENT, SMOKE ROOM, TAP ROOM, COFFEE ROOM, DINING ROOM,* KITCHEN, SCULLERY, PANTRY. GOOD CELLARAGE.

First Floor :—

CLUB ROOM (known as the "Dickens' Room"), FOUR GOOD BEDROOMS, BATH ROOM (with W.C. & Washbasin). Separate Staircase to Club Room.

The OUTBUILDINGS include :—Gent's Convenience, Empties Store, GARAGE for 2 Cars, Stabling for 4 Horses, with Loft (could be converted into a good Garage)

Well-Kept KITCHEN GARDEN with choice Fruit Trees.

The whole property extends to about

1 rood 13 perches

COMPANY'S WATER. :: COMPANY'S GAS.
MAINS ELECTRIC SUPPLY. MAIN DRAINAGE.

The Inn occupies a conspicuous Corner Position and there is ample space for extension..

FREEHOLD AND FREE FROM GROUND RENT.

Particulars of sale, for the estate of Sir F.H. Goldney, Bart, (deceased), 19 September 1941. The Hare and Hounds was bought by Mr Fussell in September 1941. He installed Fred and Grace Pullen as landlords (they had been blitzed at The Globe in Bristol). They remained at The Hare and Hounds for twenty-five years. In 1942 work commenced on building 'prefabs' for BAC personnel and a frequent bus service was provided for them. The pub frequently ran dry due to the hundreds of Irish employed in the building trade. Personnel from the three services also swelled the population. Their daughter, Phyllis, recalls tanks continually running up and down Pickwick, damaging kerbs.

41

A mail coach at 6.00 p.m. on 1 August 1984, photographed by Les Davis. In August 1784 John Palmer planned an experimental run from Bath to London. This photograph of the re-enactment was taken as it turned from Pickwick Road into Pickwick, following a change of horses. John Drayne was the guard and post horn player.

The Spread Eagle. Just before war broke out in 1914, John Edward Dyke left the Bradford on Avon Brewery to open his own retail house in Pickwick, known as the 'Spread Eagle'. Mr and Mrs Dyke managed this house for over forty years and moved to Pickwick Road upon retirement. The pub then became the 'Two Pigs'. This is another high quality photograph from the NMRC collection which they received in December 1951.

The plan of Pickwick Brewery, orignally built in 1804. This area is now a boatyard with other light industrial use.

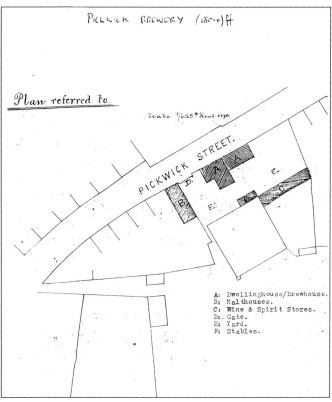

A: Dwellinghouse/Brewhouse.
B: Malthouses.
C: Wine & Spirit Stores.
D: Gate.
E: Yard.
F: Stables.

Richard Reynolds, 1735–1816. A reproduction of an engraving published in London by William Hobday. Richard was a pupil at the Friends School, Pickwick (now the Masonic Lodge). In *The Quakers of Melksham 1669-1950*, Harold Fassnidge tells us 'in youth Reynolds was not always as peaceable and well behaved as the elders would like....he set out with a gang to raid, on some pretext, the Church of England School (Dame Margarets?) but they were received so kindly by the Anglicans that their aggression evaporated and they came away friends'.

Mr and Mrs James Batley of Priory
Farm, Pickwick. The Batley family had
been farmers for generations. James'
father, John, farmed at Sheldon Manor
for twenty-one years before coming to
Corsham to farm at Pockeridge about
1889. Between leaving the farm at
Sheldon and taking over Pockeridge he
was a temporary inn keeper at The Duke
of Cumberland in Priory Street. His son,
James, opened a dairy shop around 1910
on the corner of High Street and Priory
Street. In 1928 he left the dairy shop to
take on dairy farming at Priory Farm. After
his death his daughter Joan carried on the
Dairy business. Joan's daughter, Sonia,
upon her mother's retirement (managing a
guest house at The Parsonage in Pickwick)
traded for a time under her married name,
King, until the dairy was taken over by
a Melksham businessman in the mid-
1930s, thus bringing to a close a century of
service by this family concern.

Milkmaid Joan Batley at the Dairy in Pickwick in the 1930s.

Carnival time, *c.* 1960.

The Parsonage, Pickwick. Note the stone cross atop the front gable and also above the tower. The entrance to the dairy can be seen quite clearly defined on the right hand verge.

Sperring Garage, Pickwick, c. 1920. Mr W. Sperring is on the right of the picture; his assistant Mr Hemmings of Broadstone (whose brother Gerald was also a motor mechanic) is sitting and Mr Sperring's brother-in-law, Harry Batley, is in the centre. Note the 1920s style pump. Mr Sperring Senior came from Salisbury to Pickwick during 1922 and both he and his son Hugh saw many changes in fashions and style of motor during their seventy-five years as motor engineers in Pickwick.

Four

Cross Keys, Hartham and Weavern

The Cross Keys, c. 1904. Could this be a Monday wash day? In this view, childhood appears to be quiet, safe and independent.

The Fever House (centre), *c.* 1900.

The Bath Road near the junction with Hartham Lane, *c.* 1910. A pony and trap can just be seen in the middle distance.

Weavern Farm, from the Spackman 'picnic series', c. 1910. An idyllic home, its isolation making it more suited to life with a horse and cart.

Weavern picnic, c. 1935. Here we see Reg Say with his niece Joan Say, friend Betty Archard and Joan Sheppard of Gastard. A photograph such as this could doubtless be found in the album of every Corsham family. Weavern was such a popular place to swim and picnic before the days of the swimming pool in Beechfield Road.

Weavern, *c.* 1910. This is photograph no.1 in the Spackman picnic series. One scene which blessedly has remained unchanged over the years.

Hartham Church, as built in 1862. A copy of a postcard in the Civic Society's collection.

Au Revoir, Hartham House, *c.* 1910. Photograph from the NMRC collection taken by Mrs Rupert Lycett Green. This could well record the occasion when Sir John and Lady Dickson-Poynder, he newly enobled as Lord Islington, were leaving to travel to New Zealand where he was to take up his position as Governor. He never returned to Hartham Park.

According to the reverse of this photograph this is a 'Corsham cricketing family', *c.* 1868. However, it is believed to be the 'Rowland Brotherhood' cricket team. The father was a Brunel engineer who came to Chippenham and opened the first foundry. He lived at Orwell House (now Barretts furnishers) and with his ten sons formed a prestigious local family cricket team. Perhaps the records of the Corsham Cricket Club would indicate the number of times they played at the Corsham ground and who won! A victory against Chippenham 1st XI is recorded!

A child of Hartham House, Joan Poynder. Party wear for the fashion conscious young lady. The only child of Hartham Park, Joan Dickson-Poynder, was born in 1897. She later became Lady Altrincham. Her father, Sir John Dickson-Poynder inherited a baronetcy from one uncle and s fortune from another. He had no male heir and the great Victorian and Edwardian estate of Hartham Park came to an end.

Bobby Somerset, a cousin of the present Duke of Beaufort, and Joan at the beach at Filey.

Five

Gastard

The Harp and Crown, *c.* 1904.

Outside the Harp and Crown, *c.* 1920. Note the 'Yorks' (bands that hitched trousers just below the knee) which distinguished the quarrymen (miners) from the masons. On the far left is Philip Lawence and fourth from the right is Roger Lodge (with pipe).

This photograph has been identified as Pictor's Eastlays quarry, outside the stables. The Gangers (foremen) wear bowler hats. The pickers wear soft caps to reduce head contact with the stone ceilings. Top row: William Shepard, -?-, -?-, William Lodge, Elisha Howlett. Middle row, second on the left is Frank 'Freddie' Poulsom and on the far right is Tommy Morris who had but one arm.

54

R DENT & SCHOOL GIRLS (GASTARD) JUNE 24, 1913. (SPACKMAN.)

A Spackman print of Mr Dent and
school girls at Gastard School, 24 June
1913. Unfortunately there is no record
of the names of these stylish girls.

The water tower atop Velley Hill,
demolished sometime around the
1960s. (A more accurate date would be
gratefully received!)

MR ALDERMAN FOWLER, M.P.

Pict Box L4/16 [no negative]
Robert Fowler (1828–1891)

Mr Alderman Fowler MP, (later Sir Robert Fowler) 1828–1891, who inherited Elm Grove in 1862. He demolished the family's original home and built Gastard House. Again, the authors would recommend Harold Fassnidge's prize-winning book, *The Quakers of Melksham*.

A pen and ink drawing of Gastard House by Jane Townsend of Bradford on Avon.

Six

Monks Chapel, Monks Lane

Monks Chapel in 1986. A pen and ink drawing by V.J. Wolford of Corsham.

The interior of the eyebrow window, Monks Chapel. 'It is a good thing to give thanks unto the Lord and to sing praises unto thy name O most high'. Ps 92. 1.

Monks Chapel in a photograph taken by T. C. Burnard, showing the fine original furniture which has remained virtually unchanged in 300 years.

Detailed photographs of a hinge and three-pegged timber support to the gallery, May 1972.

The interior looking west showing the depth of the gallery and pegged support on the left of the picture. Both photographs on this page are taken from the Wiltshire Buildings Record.

An oblique view of the chapel. Note the sundial above the door. Photograph by T.C. Burnard.

The story of George Gay and Thomas Hawkes

Thomas Hawkes was an estate agent, auctioneer and surveyor in the town of Williton, Somerset. He was born a few miles away at Wiveliscombe on the 3 November 1780. His firm is listed in trade directories in the years 1840 and 1842. In 1853 he appears to have taken his son into the business, although later entries show the business reverted to its original name.

Thomas Hawkes had other interests in life. He was an author and published a book entitled An Introduction to Divine Service which was printed in Watchet. This was a step away from his other great passion, music. To this end he toured Somerset and Wiltshire looking for composers of religious music, mostly amateur.

At the Independent Chapel at Corsham (Monks), he found his champion. George Gay the organist, had composed and published many hymns in his time. He was also an innovator. He abandoned the use of the usual signatures at the beginning of each treble and bass clef and devised one of his own, based on the key of 'G'.

Thomas Hawkes published his life's work in 1833. It was called the Hawkes Psalmony, printed in Watchet and contained about two hundred tunes. It featured many of George Gay's tunes. Gay had the habit of naming his tunes after local villages such as Neston, Chapel Knapp, Monks, Patterdown and Corsham. The author of Fifty Psalms and Hymn Tunes he revised and corrected the whole of Thomas Hawkes' Psalmony which says much for Hawkes confidence in George Gay. Hawkes was a man of very definite views on the rendering of church music, which he elaborates in the preface to his volume. His most notable advice is, in so many words: 'If you can't sing...shut up!' Thomas Hawkes died at Williton in 1858.

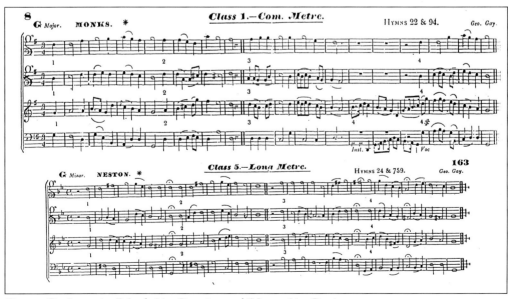

George Gay's music, 'Monks' in G major and 'Neston' in G minor.

An original Spackman photograph of Monks Chapel, 23 June 1936. Back left corner: -?-, Joan Poulsom (nee Hillier), -?-, Mrs Poulsom. Second row: -?-, -?-, Mrs W. Knapp, Mrs Lawrence, -?-, -?-, Mrs Freegard, Mrs Burchell, -?-, -?-, Mrs Simmons, -?-, -?-. Front row, on the left: Maurice Knapp. Seated Revd Jones Congregational Minister of Corsham.

A memorial stone set into the wall in Monks Lane. This was dedicated to a James Porter, who was 'killed by a horse' in 1785.

Seven

Easton, The Ridge and Neston

The Whores Pond at The Ridge, Neston, *c.* 1970. Local historian, John Poulsom, delighted in describing the need for and use of this quiet pond, home to moorhen and coot. It is hard to believe it was deep enough to cause much anguish to any woman. Emerging from the odorous mud must surely have been the threat? What happened to the errant males? A photograph by T.C. Burnard.

At Easton, on the fringe of Corsham Park lived the Gifford family who farmed and trained teams of shire horses. In this photograph we see Richard Gifford with children Sarah and John with D. Taylor, the herdsman, and their two shires. His wife, Angela is driving the two Shetland ponies and Linda Best. Their home at the time, Easton Court Farm, in the background.

Beatrice and William (Bill) Watts at the gate of their cottage home in Chapel Lane, 1908. Note the thatch.

Mr and Mrs G.P. Fuller, on the occasion of their golden wedding anniversary, January 1914.

The family gathering at Neston Park to celebrate the golden wedding, January 1914. Mr Fuller had the needs of the villagers at heart and in 1906, opened a glove factory in a barn at Brockleaze to provide employment.

The Glove Factory Cricket Team, *c.* 1930. The Glove Factory was bounded on one side by an orchard and it is there the team practised in their lunch hour. On the left are: George Dyke, Len Scott, Sid Cook?, Bill Gale, Ern Helps, ? Hiscocks. Front row: Bill Watts, -?-, -?-, Wilf Light (capt), Coopy White, Tom ?

Neston Institute Football Club, champions of the Melksham league, 1926/27.

A hay wain, decorated for the fete at Neston Park, *c.* 1930. It is leaving Pitts Farm, previously known as 'Ducks'(that being the farmers name) and then 'Orms'. The horse 'Blossom' is led by Frank Harding.

Nellie Gibbons (see page 33) by the barn in Elley Green, April 1931. Nellie was a champion butter maker and used to cycle to both Neston Park and Jaggards to make their butter. Her father George had a small holding of thirteen and a half acres where the Leafield estate now stands. The barn on the left was used as a café in the Second World War. An Australian, Geoffrey Benstead, cooked great dishes of sausage and mash and chunky sandwiches for the immigrant workers. The barn was demolished in the mid-1990s and four houses have now been built on the paddock.

Pool Green on the day the railway line became a river, 25 June 1935. Geoff Knapp recalls his father had to come and fetch him from school in the hay wagon, the water lay so deep on the lanes.

Stanley Gibbons at Leafield Farm in a photograph taken by Nellie Gibbons, 1935. The Ministry of Defence requisitioned the land in the 1939/45 war and prefabs were erected as homes for the Irish workers. It is now a trading estate.

Doris and Peter Jackson who settled into country life with glee, *c.* 1940. Such were the numbers that Capt. Druitt and the staff at Neston School arranged to teach the two groups separately. Many families formed strong bonds with their 'guests' and have kept in touch to this day.

Fred and Linda Hales, *c.* 1930. They ran the Neston Club from 1946 until their retirement.

Jaggards, from the NMRC collection, sometime around 1853-61. This house has a fascinating history. It was once home to a notorious family of highwaymen in the sixteenth century.

Chrissie Poulsom's cows lumbering along the lane with the 'Old Vicarage' visible across the fields, c. 1990. The village no longer benefits from their twice daily traffic calming qualities.

Florence Light (nee Barnett) 'The Angel' of Neston, c. 1902. She was an outstanding character who brought generations of Neston children into the world and nursed them and their families when they were ill. No lane was too dark nor quarry too deep to stop her fulfilling her calling. As a child she lived with her family at Staverton, attending the National School. At the age of nine she entered service, looking after children until she was eighteen. She then travelled to Lancashire to train in her chosen profession, returning to the West Country to study maternity work at Kingswood, Bristol. She and her husband Wilf Light married in 1905 and furnished their home for 12s. 6d. They had two children, Grace and Francis at Bakers Corner.

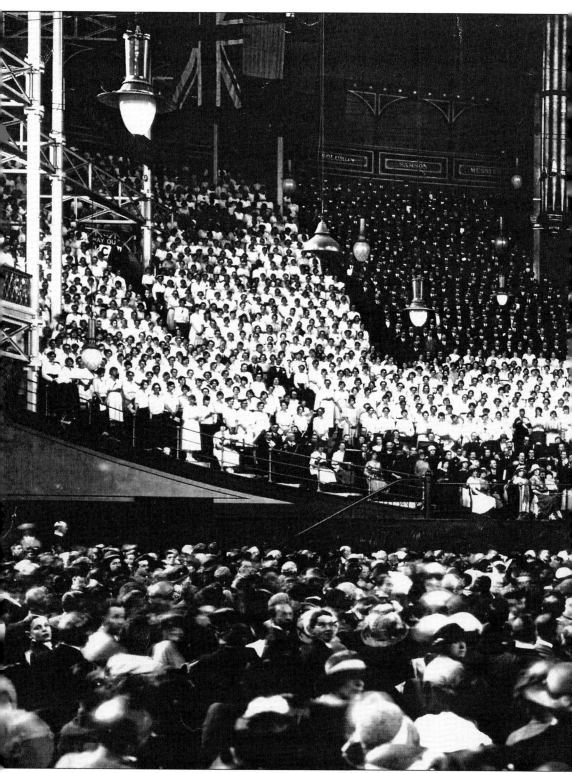

Crystal Palace, *c.* 1922. On this grand occasion the contingent from Corsham is beneath 'Judas

Maccabeus' to the right of the organ.

A visit to Bath entailed a walk across Kingsdown to the Bathford Inn, and a trolley ride. Florence and daughter Grace (on the right) shopping in Bath, c. 1930.

A choir outing to Cheddar, c. 1920. Wilfred Light arranged the yearly choir outings. A keen singer he sang in both the Neston Chapel Choir and the Corsham Congregational Choir. The lady (top right) apparently complained on her return to Neston that there was a large hole in the skirt of her coat due to the vibration of the solid wheels on the rough roads!

Neston School, c. 1921. Grace Light did not have happy memories of her earliest schooldays. She was under four years old and would run home to Bakers Corner and hide beneath the bed! The teacher was stern and hasty with her hand if you hesitated over an answer. First writing lessons were carried out in a tray of sand. The photograph shows Mrs Mansfield on the right (who was an excellent, gentle teacher). The headmaster's wife, Mrs Inkpen, is on the left. Back row: Betty Sawyer, Nina May, Cissy Dyke, Frances Butter, Carrie ?, Ruby Eddolls, Violet May, Gwen Sheppard, Hilda Hancock,. Middle row: Doris Blake, Blanche Baker, Alice Blake, Dolly Sawyer, Joyce Eddolls, Phillis Dyke, Freda Way, Nellie May. Front row: Visitor, Babs Eddolls, Nora Sawyer, Dolly Dyke, Margery May, Grace Light, Chrissie Webb, Nancy Seymour, (Sands Farm).

The girls of Corshamside (Neston) School working in the sunken gardens.

The boys tended the vegetable garden. They grew every type of fruit and vegetable and it was an aspect of village life which the evacuees embraced with delight.

Copy of newspaper article.

Sylvan Walk, Neston's unique memorial of twenty-five years to the late King George V's reign has now been completed. 'Church Rise has been transformed by the work of the villagers led by a dedicated Jubilee Memorial Commitee which included Capt. Druitt, Col. W.F. Fuller, Mr E. Gathorne Hill, Mr Hiscocks, Mr R. Knapp, Mr F. Lilley, Mr E.S. Davis, Mr R. Hancock, Mr S. Stafford, Mr A. Higgins, Mr F. Jones, Mr G.H. Davis, Mr R. Hancock, Mr S. Stafford, Mr A. Higgins, Mr F. Jones, Mr G.H. Lawrence, Mr E. Sparkes, Mrs W. Light, Mrs A. Baker, Mrs H. Hudd, Mrs W. Moules, Mrs James Hancock (treasurer). The Corsham Town Band under Mr H. Pickett and members of the Neston British Legion under Mr H. Hiscocks awaited. There were speeches from County and Parish representatives and afterwards 300 people gathered as guests of Col. Fuller for tea in the school, the catering was done by Messrs Johnstone of Corsham. Afterwards the company availed themselves of the opportunity to inspect the school'.

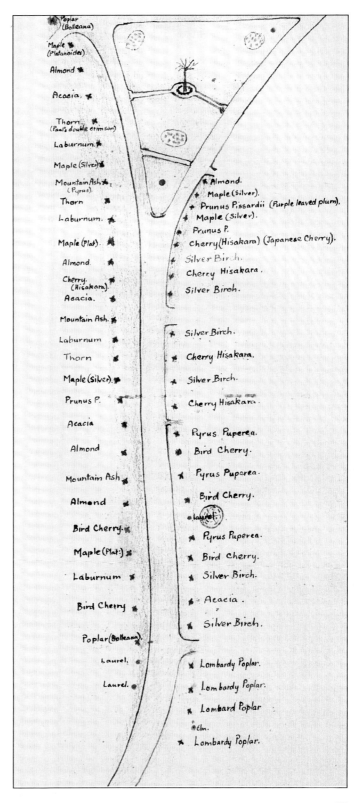

Overmoor Farm, *c.* 1988. The conversion of this old barn is considered to be the most successful in the District and became the headquarters of ESD, Energy for Sustainable Development, who operate a worldwide consultancy in renewable energy. The dovecote has a fine datestone recording that it was built in 1731 .

Fleetwood shaft and trolley lines, the last two heaps of stone waiting to be removed.

Harvest at Overmoor Farm, *c.* 1950. Left to right: Jim Townsend, -?-, farmer Christie, -?-, Tom Higgins, John and Peter Townsend, Mr Dyke, -?-.

Overmoor Farm, *c.* 1988. A tractor for each member of the family? The farm was sold, the Poulsom family moving to Wormwood Farm at Wadswick where their son continues mixed farming. The intriguing farmhouse was purchased and sensitively restored.

The porch of Great Lypiatt Farm, Neston, *c.* 1918.

Rhona Barnes with the sheep dog, *c.* 1930.

Rhona and Charlie's daughter, Vi Barnes, (later the doctors' receptionist and Superintendent of St John's) at New Grove Farm.

Harvesting, a friendly affair, c. 1940.

Maurice and Sarah Knapp, c. 1910. Great Lypiatt Farm, home to the Knapp family for three generations. Geoff Knapp's grandfather first rented the farm at the turn of the century, and was succeeded by his son Richard and wife Winifred. In 1996 Geoff and his wife June retired. Various items of ancient farming equipment were discovered at this time and donated both to the Lackham Rural Life and Avebury Museums. Long associated with the Civic Society, their yearly farm tours (trailer rides around their own and Robin Mortimer's Ridge farm) were enjoyed by hundreds of local people.

The Allen family at West Wells, c. 1915. The sailor is Leslie Allen (just sixteen years of age). The girls in front are his three sisters, the youngest of whom (Mrs Doris Sawyer) still lived, in 1997, in Neston. Leslie always walked to the railway station via Spring Lane (his sisters unable to bear the parting would hide in the copse at the corner). Eighty years later the Civic Society won funding via a Rural Action Grant to plant a mixed hedge along Pucketts Way, the new byway. Beech trees were donated and planted in Leslie Allen's memory by nephew, Bob Allen, then a society member.

Charlie Barnes at New Grove Farm, Elley Green, c. 1930. When the family came from the Isle of Wight, Charlie drove his cattle from Southampton to their new home in Neston.

Farmer Richard Knapp leaving for market from Great Lypiatt Farm, Neston, *c.* 1933.

Mechanisation comes to Great Lypiatt, *c.* 1949.

Eight

Pound Mead, Pound Pill and Station Road

Corsham people gathered for the unveiling of the war memorial at the junction of Pound Mead, Station and Stokes Road. This was the first public duty performed by Lieut. Philip Mountbatten following his engagement to Princess Elizabeth in August 1947. Photograph by William Hardwell.

Pound Mead, looking west from the engine shed, c. 1960. In the foreground is the site of the old gas works.

Valley Road, c. 1960. Pockeridge Lodge had been demolished and new housing is visible on the brow of the hill. There is a note attached to this photograph which mentions that the railway fence from Potley Bridge to the aqueduct is made of ex-GWR mainline bridge rails.

The Stone Wharves, just south of Corsham Station, in the heyday of the Corsham stone trade. The houses in The Cleeve are clearly visible in the background. The stone blocks descended to the rail sidings for shipping around the country. This photograph has been published many times, but it provides the back cloth to a tale unearthed by John Poulsom in *The Wiltshire Times & Gazette*, 12 June 1861:

'The usually quiet, sedate looking town of Corsham has seldom a more animated appearance than it wore on Monday last, on the occasion of the annual Whitsun festival of the members of what has now become an important branch of the Great Wiltshire Society. Mr Bourne (the indefatigable steward) stated at the dinner that a membership of 143 members was evidence of the improved habits of the people, both morally and socially. He said a more respectable looking body of men we have rarely seen gathered together. At a divine meeting in the parish church an excellent service was preached compressed into a short compass, and nonetheless telling on that account by Revd Mr Sargeant, one of the curates. Members headed by Mr Yockney's volunteer band marched in procession to a field (Tellcroft) on the outskirts of the town. Here an immense tent had been erected where there was a capital dinner, nicely cooked and served up hot, provided by Mr Jones of the Packhorse Inn. The company then quitted the tent and for hours afterward the adjacent field was the scene of continued mirth and amusement. Rustic sports of various kinds went on with unabated vigour, stimulated by the music of the energetic band. It was not until the moon had shed her rays on the scene that the queer old town resumed its wonted state of quiet repose.'

Pound Pill, prior to widening. During an exhibition in the library, Mrs Bullen recalled an accident on the Pound Pill bridge sometime around 1914. A pony bolted as it approached the bridge and it fell over the parapet. Luckily the wheels remained lodged against the wall but the shafts broke, the traces strangled the horse and it fell onto the line beneath. A ganger ran to the tunnel entrance to signal to the London bound train in order to prevent a derailment. When the passengers heard the story there was a collection for the driver of the trap and £76 handed to him - a great deal of money in those days.

A minature of Uriah Goold.

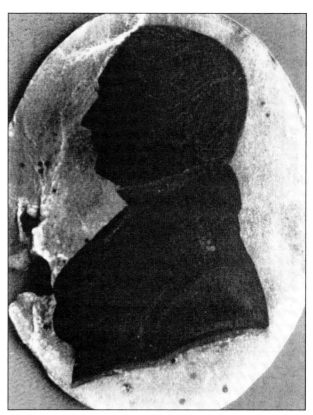

The reverse side of the above minature.

The Goold Story

Uriah Goold came to Corsham in the early 1800s. By 1830 he had established a tan yard, next to his house Ash Villa on Pound Pill, and owned a quarry. He was the co-founder of the Baptist church. One of his sons, Joseph, possessed a fine bass voice. Within the mid-Victorian 'concert circuit' he met and fell in love with a brilliant young pianist, Clara Macfarlane. She was the daughter of Major Macfarlane, an influential figure in the city of Bath and the owner of a music shop on Pulteney Bridge. At the age of nine Clara had been billed as a 'child prodigy' and performed with adult orchestras.

Joseph approached Major Macfarlane for the hand of his daughter, but was rebuffed in no uncertain terms! Clara, however, had long since tired of the pressures of her reputation and one day, on the pretext of visiting her dressmaker, she eloped with Joseph, leaving Bath forever.

The young couple set up a bookshop in Swindon. Its failure prompted a move to Nottingham and the establishment of a soft drinks plant (Joseph's invention) which also failed. It soon became apparent that Joseph, the dreamer/inventor, had little capacity for business. Clara thus became the main provider and returned to music, as a part-time teacher, to support the home and ever-increasing family.

A lifelong friendship with the Spackman family encouraged the Goolds to return to their roots at Corsham where one daughter, Daisy, had married Herbert Spackman, and ran a school. So, between the wars, came Kate and family, Amy, Edith and Bertha. Inheriting their mother's teaching talent, Edith, Bertha and Daisy produced some outstanding young pianists from generations of Corsham children. And Clara? She passed her final years living with Edith and Bertha in their little cottage in Priory Street, a stone's throw from Uriah Goold's Baptist church, until her death in 1939.

The Goold's Tanyard, Pound Pill.

An advertising poster for one of the concerts at which Joseph Goold performed.

Joseph Goold as a young man.

Clara Goold.

Joseph Goold in later years.

Priory Road (not Street). The house with the railings in the right foreground is Dill House, once called Rose Cottage and the home of Herbert Spackman. The Spackmans and Goolds were great friends and would, therefore, have been constant visitors over the years.

An interior view of Herbert Spackman's music room in Priory Street, before the Great War. Note the violin on the table in the right foreground.

Station Road Cottages, *c.* 1875. The only other buildings at that time were the chapel (1856) and the seventeenth-century cottages opposite, which are still there today. This is one half of a stereoscopic photograph, probably taken by Joseph Goold. A well in the corner of the garden, as the road bears to the left, was discovered quite recently. The cottages themselves were demolished in 1884.

Pound Pill, *c.* 1880. The name originally applied to the entire south facing escarpment and is derived from the 'Pound', an enclosure for stray animals sited in the south-west corner of the cricket field.

Floods outside the Royal Arthur public house, now the Great Western, 1967. The type of flooding that would have the drain covers lifting in the tan yard fields!

A Spackman original of the Royal Defence Corps, during the First World War. The undergrowth and undulating surroundings suggest that this may have been taken in The Batters.

Nine

The School Room, Almshouses and Corsham Lake

Springtime at the Almshouses, *c.* 1948.

Joseph and Emma Crosse, wardens from 1874–1916. Mr Joseph Crosse and his wife are the first wardens it has been possible to trace and they were in residence for the greatest number of years. Mr Crosse was active in the town and was elected to sit at petty sessions. He was on the committee of the Mechanics Institute; foreman of the jury on a number of suspicious sudden deaths. He was overseer at vestry meetings at which the rate was set and in 1889 applied to the Board of Trade to supply water at Corsham. He was also treasurer of the Corsham Cycling Club which was formed in 1889.

An etching of the gates and porch of the Warden's House by E. Chigwell.

Jesse Say in uniform during the First World War. By trade he was a painter and decorator and he married Amy Crosse, daughter of Joseph and Emma. Together they would run dances at the British Legion and sometimes the town hall. He was the MC and she played the piano.

Amy with firstborn, a daughter, Eileen. Amy was a great churchgoer and Sunday school teacher. Two sons Jack and Clement both sang in the choir. On Sundays, on some occasions before they sat down to their meal, the children would have to go out and deliver dinners to any deserving lady at the Almshouses. They lived at No. 30 Station Road.

The schoolroom pulpit and master's chair.

A Spackman original of the Almshouse residents, with a total of 516 years between them. Their ages are, from left to right: 92, 89, 87, 87, 83, 78. The lady in black with the light-edged shawl was Mrs Plumb.

Corsham Town Band, c. 1926. The Society have many photographs of events at which the Corsham Band were performing. Formed over 140 years ago, they play at local fetes, concerts, private and public functions and now meet to practice in the church of St Philip & St James, Neston. They have an extensive repertoire and travel widely to perform, with success, in various competitions. If you play a brass instrument, why not join them? See their website: www.corshamband.com

Corsham Town Band, marching past Chippenham Town Hall.

Herbert Spackman's little joke! A special bus service was run from Bath for the skaters wishing to get to Corsham Lake. So many people came that you could hear the 'hum' of the skates in the High Street. In his diaries, Herbert Spackman refers to the 'Corsham Pond' and there are references to Charles Mayo having fallen through the ice on two occasions, on 19 January 1880 and 13 January 1881. In this photograph Herbert superimposed the bus on the lake!

A photograph taken by Spackman of a gospel group, 23 July 1915

Corsham Fire Brigade Services. On 1 June 1895, the newly formed parish council was empowered to engage twelve part-time firemen at two shillings (24 old pence) annually. A blacksmith by profession, Mr John Ball, described as a huge, larger-than-life figure of a man was appointed. He was known as a kindly and respected official. The parish council was obliged to increase the fireman's pay to three shillings (36 old pence) annually because of extra practices and maintenance of the engine (mechanical pump). This same year a big fire at the Station Hotel destroyed the stabling which housed up to forty horses. All were rescued from the inferno. It was reported to the council in October 1896 that the brigade bill of £3. 15s had not been paid in respect of their work dousing the fire at Station Hotel. Many tradesmen, shopkeepers and their employees were members of Corsham Fire Brigade. Notable captains were: Alfred Butt, a tailor, Arthur J. Hobbs, a saddler. The photograph is believed to be the first of its kind depicting Corsham Parish Fire Brigade. It must also be remembered that not only were the brigade part-time, but the horses required to pull the tender had to be caught or unhitched from the baker or corn merchant's carts.

The entrance to the old fire engine station in Priory Street.

Ten

Around High Street and Market Square

The southern end of the High Street, *c.* 1903. Corsham Post Office at that time can be seen in the foreground to the right.

Parkside was for a time the home of architect, Harold Brakespear, knighted for his work on Windsor Castle. It was later the home of Sir Michael Tippett who composed many major works in the magnificent music room overlooking the garden. These included four symphonies, operas, string quartets and piano sonatas – works that have acquired world-wide recognition such as The Midsummer Marriage and The Knot Garden. During the seventies the High Street suffered much upheaval and the construction of a car park to the south of the garden caused Sir Michael to seek a more peaceful environment.

Gracie and Nettie of No.7 High Street. In 1906 William King of Chippenham appointed two of his daughters to take charge of his Corsham branch. They cycled to Corsham in the summer and used the pony and trap in the winter. Nettie, on the right, was well-known locally as a singer. She married Mr H.R. James who at that time happened to be the manager of an opposing ironmongery business in Chippenham.

G. D. Crook, Wholesale and Retail Drapery, Millinery, Outfitting, and Boot Establishment, High Street, Corsham. —Dating back in its foundation to a period between thirty-five and forty years, and promoted for some years under the auspices of a Mr. J. C. Child, this comprehensive business came under its present enterprising proprietor some eight years ago, and made such rapid strides that about three years since Mr. Crook found it necessary to annex "London House" adjoining, so that his premises now present a most attractive frontage of four spacious show windows, altogether about sixty feet in extent. Withindoors all the appointments of the place are in the best modern style, while everywhere there are evidences of the care and attention bestowed by the proprietor in arranging for the prompt service

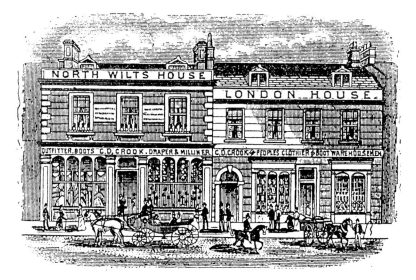

and general comfort and convenience, not only of patrons, but of his numerous staff of courteous and capable assistants. Every department of general drapery, millinery and millinery materials, and fancy drapery goods, household linens, heavy goods, and kindred commodities, ladies' *lingerie*, babylinen, and children's underwear, gentlemen's outfitting items, hosiery, corsets, and gloves, bespoke clothing, boots and shoes, and haberdashery, and all manner of smallwares are exhaustively represented, and are particularly rich in the best and most fashionable novelties; while large stocks are maintained to meet the demands of a good wholesale connection and the orders arriving from the firm's two country travellers. In the executive departments for millinery and tailoring only expert hands are employed, and all orders are executed in a prompt and satisfactory manner. Personally Mr. Crook is well known and much esteemed amongst a very large local *clientèle*, both trade and family, as an enterprising and thoroughly capable business man.

G. D. Crook, wholesale and retail drapery, c. 1890. This was taken from a trade journal.

F. Lord tobacconists, c. 1963. In the early thirties Frederick Lord followed Mr Edward Powell as the new proprietor of the shop. During the mid-1950s, Mr Lord stocked many Corgi miniature models of Second World War vehicles including tanks and lorries. These are now highly valued collector's items. The shop is now an opticians.

Birds, confectioners, c. 1905. These premises housed Barclays Bank for many years but despite protestations, the bank closed and the property was sold. Julie Kent Interiors moved in but Perfect Rooms now occupies the building.

Francis Baines (and John Baines before him) traded as chemists, stationers, booksellers and bottled wines from the mid-1870s in the High Street until the early 1920s.

Herbert Baines grocers shop in Pickwick Road.

Herbert Baines traded as a grocer in Pickwick Road and a confectioner in the High Street. He was secretary to the Corsham Gas Company and also secretary to the Corsham Waterworks Ltd from 1920 until the outbreak of the Second World War. The family photograph shows Phylis and Edith (Mrs Goddard) who were aunts to the baby, Edna, in christening robes held by her grandmother, Mrs F. Baines. Mrs Ethel Baines, mother of Edna, is on her left. A family with over 125 years service to Corsham and District. Edna became Mrs E. Beavers of Corshamside Dairies,

Miss Emily Bartlett from Biddestone. She was a servant to the Baines family, c. 1910.

This picture was taken *c.* 1923. Joe James is standing with his father Mr H.R. James, outside their shop at the southern end of the High Street.

Bromley's builders yard, *c.* 1880. Note the chimneys of High Street properties in the background. This area later became a stone yard, a coal merchant's yard and from 1925 was used as a centre for taxi hire and garaging by Mr Giles and Carl Buckle. Later still it was the site of the former Gateway Supermarket and is now the Co-operative Supermarket in the newly refurbished and repaved Martingate Centre.

The ornate early Victorian porch to the side of No.25 High Street.

The old wrought iron gate and gate posts to No. 25. The date and their present whereabouts is unknown.

In this photograph Richard Morling has captured Post Office Lane prior to the demolition of Hancocks' yard and cottage home, 1960.

This building, of such quality, was demolished.

Corsham in mourning – the military funeral of Pte. R.Brown on 26 October 1915. This photograph was taken by Herbert Spackman from an upper window of his parents' home.

Corsham Church Lads Brigade, *c.* 1909, led by the bearded Sgt Hawthorn.

A drawing by Oswald Brakspear of the Poor House, 1728–1836. Damaged by fire, the Civic Society fought hard to raise awareness and funds to restore the building. It is now E.S. Electrical with a modern, plate glass window - previously the North Wilts Meat Co.

Gone, gone gone! A photograph of Catherine Court taken from the Malthouse flats at the rear of No.70, looking south. No wonder Corsham is bereft of quaint mews areas in which to site a café or group of mutually supportive shops.

A. Matthew, draper, milliner, outfitter and tailor. This splendid shop occupied double frontage. According to Kelly's Directory he traded from the early 1890s for twenty years. His shop has changed hands several times since. Confectioner, tobacconist, a corn dealers, dyers and cleaners, and the gas board showroom have all occupied the premises. As the twentieth century closed it was part social and games club and a veterinary health centre.

Mr Field, who sold tobacco, stationery and fancy goods, c. 1910.

Mr Bowerbank's garage in the High Street, c. 1932. He is pictured on the right beside the pump talking with Mr Palmer who ran a car hire business in Pickwick Road.

South African soldiers marching into Corsham, *c.* 1900.

Left, right, left, right, up the High Street.

The junction of High Street and Priory Street, photographed before the building of the Mayo Memorial in 1897. The eight houses in the centre of the picture have been known as the Flemish Buildings since the late nineteenth and early twentieth century, although why this should be remains a mystery.

An early twentieth-century photograph of the Flemish Buildings and Mayo memorial fountain built by public subscription to commemorate Charles Mayo (1834–95) who undertook many good works for Corsham, especially the bringing of clean running water to the town in 1889. A bid for Heritage Lottery Funding by Peter Tapscott in 2006 led to its refurbishment in 2007 by stonemason, Rob Fleming. See the Civic Society's website for the full story of this undertaking.

The Corsham Corn Stores, *c.* 1960.

The Coffee Bar at the Town Hall, *c.* 1900. This print is from an original Brakspear negative.

CLOSING DAY OF HOSPITAL AUG 30, 1919

The Town Hall was used as a hospital during the First World War. Mr Daymond's father is second from the right in the front row. Mr Jennings (in the wheelchair on the left) lived at Ashford Cottages, Priory Street, after the war. Mr Ernest Merrett and Mr Percy Gane were Quartermasters to the hospital.

The Town Hall staged craft exhibitions, c. 1880. This is a print from a glass negative.

The Town Hall was also used as a theatre. This is a picture of the Dramatic Society's fancy dress ball in 1939. The last social event of 'Old Corsham' held on the eve of the outbreak of the Second World War. Back row: Philip Doel, Mrs Box, Edna Grey, Joe James, Harry Andrews, Geoffery Moore, Betty Wood, Mrs Currie, Miss Wood, Ms Baker, Mrs Trout, Miss Swift. Middle row: Herbert Head, Mrs Head, Margaret Harvey, Marjorie White, -?-, -?-, Muriel Trait, Joan James. Front row: Graham Allen, Ken Davis, Queenie Coates, Ethel Barker (nee Smith) Muriel Freeth, Marjorie Davis.

This photograph was thought to commemorate the retirement of Lewin Spackman as Corsham coroner, but may more likely be the occasion of his retirement as Clerk to the Parish Council. He served in this position from its inception in 1895 until his retirement in 1923. Back row: -?-, -?-, Mr Bird, -?-, Mr Batley. Middle row: Miss Tennant, -?-, -?-. Front row: -?-, Lewin Spackman, Henry Burgess, Jesse Fido, H.B. Coates.

A Spackman photograph of the Women's Suffrage Pilgrimage as it arrived outside the Town Hall in Corsham on 16 July, 1913, en route from Land's End to London.

Miss Frances Strerling speaking to the crowds in Corsham during the Women's Suffrage Pilgrimage from Land's End to London on 16 July, 1913, recorded by Herbert Spackman.

Church Street from Church Square, *c.* 1910. This area of the town is now popular with producers of TV period dramas.

A photograph taken by Spackman of the Red Cross sale held in the Market Square, the year of the Great War, 1915.

Mr Heavens, a retired postman and self-taught artist, lived in the Flemish buildings in the 1960s. In this photograph he is shown displaying his bird's eye view of Princes Street, Edinburgh. Photograph by R. Eden.

Another early postcard view of the Flemish houses. The sets of bay windows were added to the original fifteenth-century house on the left in 1632. The lord of the manor had the owners fined, arguing successfully that they encroached onto his land.

The view from the church spire (if you dared to keep your eyes open!) in a photograph taken by John Logan, *c*. 1938.

The 'Cradle of Corsham'. (NMRC) An oblique view.

ALTUS - High Up and Deep Down in Corsham

The ALTUS works (in war YMCA)
Gave welcome then to the ordnance servicemen,
To sailors trained to serve on sea or shore,
To airmen sweeping skies by night and day.
And when the conflict ended, refugees
from central Europe came to find a home
to pause at West Wells, no more forced to roam
lost victims of tyrannical decrees.
Our servicemen and women, back in swarms,
found work: some banker-masons 'neath the sky
dependent on stone-cutters underground
in cavern-stores some laboured, some on farms.
Of such, from far and wide and deep and high,
was shaped the Corsham that today is found.

by the Rev. Canon Mervyn Drewett, Rector of Greater Corsham, 1980–1994.
Winner of the 1997 Corsham Festival Poetry Competition

Acknowledgements

In the foreward, Tom Burnard refers to our indebtedness to those two early Corsham photographers, Herbert Spackman and Harold Brakspear, and to the generosity of their families. Richard Morling's contribution in the 1960s has also been utilised in compiling this book and thanks are due to Ex Libris Press for allowing us to quote from The Quakers of Melksham on two occasions; also Jane Townsend for permission to use her line drawing of Gastard House and Vic Wolford his pen and ink drawing of Monks Chapel. The photograph of the engraving of Richard Reynolds has been produced by courtesy of the Library Committee of Friends House, London. The National Monuments Record Centre, Swindon, have also been kind enough to allow us to reproduce photographs from their collection, some of these the property of the Wiltshire Buildings Record.

We are also most grateful to the families who have entrusted us with their treasured photographs, Joan Webb (nee Batley), Cynthia Merrett, Joan Moon, Margaret Hancock, Geoff Knapp, Alan Denhard, Bob Allen, Angela Gifford, Mrs Arthur Gingell, Norman Duckworth, Jean Hartley. Grace Holland, Phyllis Cox, Nell Logan, Nellie Thomas, Winnie Weeks and Pat Whalley; Jack Archer and Mervyn Tyte for their photographs of the Choral Challenge Shield and Spring Lane and Clive Hancock for the fascinating photographs on pages 4, 26, 90, 109, 114, and 123.

Without the painstaking research of Joe James we would not have been able to print either the Goold story or that of Thomas Hawkes and George Gay, the latter with the assistance of staff at the Somerset County Archives. Indeed, Joe James, Les Davis and Pat Whalley have all researched and contributed to the content and are deserving of heartfelt thanks.

Anne Lock 1997

The first volume was compiled in 1997 and reprinted in 2006. This third edition benefits from a thorough proof reading by Peter French of The Corsham Bookshop, Pat Whalley and Michael Rumsey. I am also indebted to Dr Negley Harte, Hon. Fellow and Hon. Research Fellow in History, University College London, who effortlessly corrected dates and contributed materially to the quality of the captions.